TRADITIONS AND CELEBRATIONS

PURIM

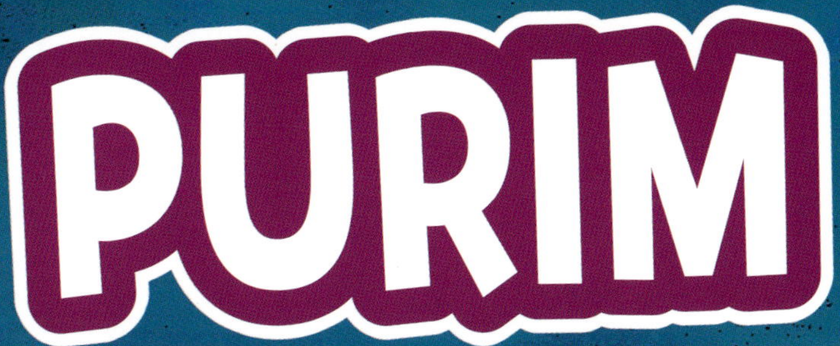

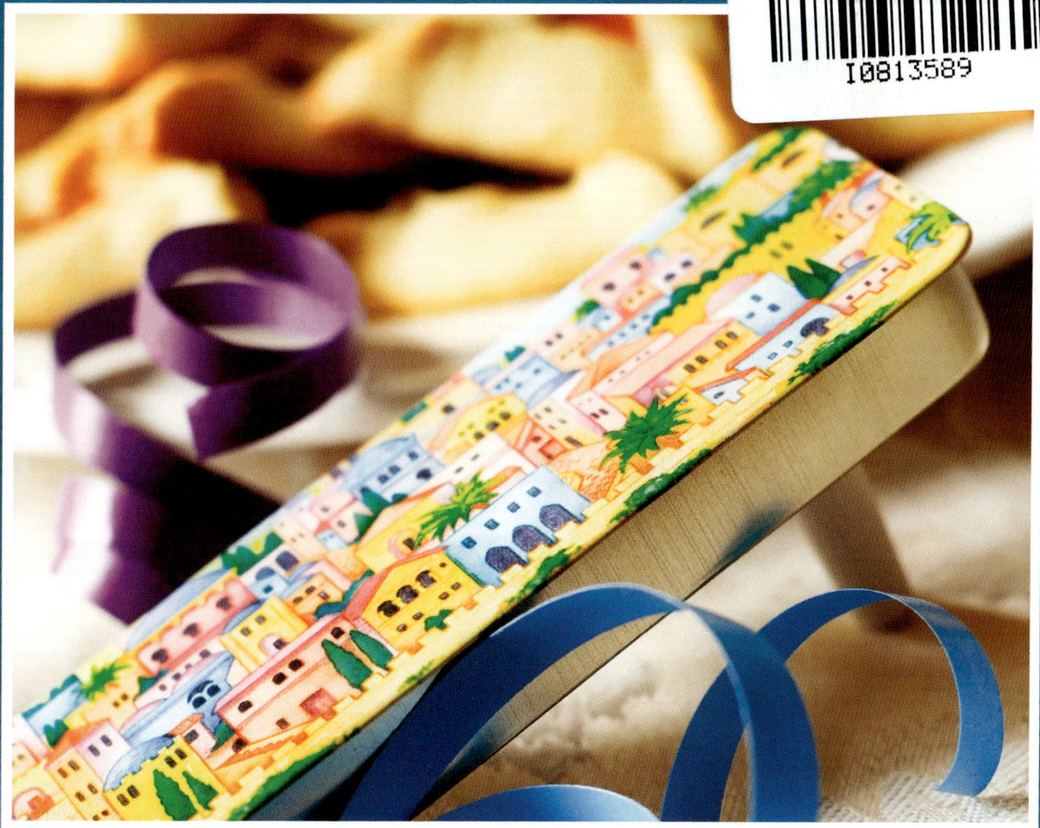

by Emily Raij

PEBBLE
a capstone imprint

Published by Pebble, an imprint of Capstone
1710 Roe Crest Drive, North Mankato, Minnesota 56003
capstonepub.com

Library of Congress Cataloging-in-Publication Data is available on the Library of Congress website.
ISBN: 9798875284458 (hardcover)
ISBN: 9798875284403 (paperback)
ISBN: 9798875284410 (ebook PDF)

Summary: Readers will discover the many ways Jewish people celebrate the Purim holiday, from helping people in need to sharing a meal.

Editorial Credits
Editor: Carrie Sheely; Designer: Heidi Thompson; Media Researcher: Rebekah Hubstenberger; Production Specialist: Tori Abraham

Image Credits
Getty Images: Dan Kitwood, 13, duncan1890, 6, iStock/500, 21, iStock/BibleArtLibrary, 9, iStock/chameleonseye, 16, 17, Nathan Bilow, 28, Patricia Marroquin, 12, Rafael Ben-Ari, 25, The Washington Post, 19; Newscom: Debbie Noda/Modesto Bee/ZUMAPRESS, 5, Eugene Garcia/ZUMA Press, 14, Melissa Lyttle/Tampa Bay Times/ZUMAPRESS, 10, Richard Tsong-Taatarii/ZUMA Press, 15; Shutterstock: blueeyes, cover, 1, bonchan, 11, Danny Smythe, 26, Elena Rostunova, 23, Elzbieta Sekowska, 27, Marta Maziar, 22, Nigmatulina Aleksandra, 29, Viktoria Hodos, 20

Design Elements
Shutterstock: Rafal Kulik

Printed and bound in China. 006459

TABLE OF CONTENTS

Words in **bold** are in the glossary.

What Is Purim?

Kids dress up in costumes. They read and listen to a story. They act out parts of it. People shake noisemakers. Families give baskets of food to each other. They help those in need. It is Purim!

Purim is a Jewish holiday. It celebrates when the Jews in Persia stopped a plan to destroy them many years ago. Purim is a festive time. The Jewish people **rejoice** that good won over hate.

Jews go to synagogue to read the story about how their people were saved long ago.

Queen Esther begs the king not to carry out the plans to kill the Jews.

In the 400s BCE, the Persian king was married to Queen Esther. She was Jewish but didn't tell the king about her background. The king had a helper named Haman. Haman wanted power. He wanted everyone in the kingdom to bow down to him.

Queen Esther's cousin Mordecai refused. This made Haman angry. He planned to kill all the Jews. Queen Esther found out about Haman's plan. She **convinced** the king to stop Haman. Queen Esther saved the Jewish people.

When Is Purim?

Purim gets its name from the **Hebrew** word meaning “lots.” Lots are objects in a group. People draw lots to make a choice. Haman drew lots to choose the day for his evil plan. It was the 14th day of the Hebrew month of Adar. Today, it is when Jews celebrate Purim.

Jewish holidays are based on a **lunar** calendar. It follows the phases of the moon. That means holiday dates change each year. Purim usually falls in February or March.

The story of Esther says that the queen and other Jews celebrated after the king decided to protect them.

Purim lasts two days. Jews may go to **synagogue**. They read and listen to the story of Esther to remember her **bravery**.

Colorful costumes can stand out among the people at synagogue on Purim.

The story is called the Megillah. It is read once at night and once during the day. When Haman's name is read aloud, people boo or shake noisemakers called groggers.

How Do People Celebrate Purim?

Purim feels like a party! People have been celebrating it for thousands of years. Children and adults enjoy dressing up as people from the Purim story. Everyone has fun acting out the story. Kids may also play games.

Children in costumes for Purim

People use creativity as they act out Purim spiels.

There are four **commandments**, or mitzvot, Jewish people should follow on Purim. One is hearing the story of Esther. Many people go to synagogue to hear the story. They also act it out like a play. They might add silly voices or music. The play is called a Purim spiel.

Purim spiels can include dancing and costume themes.

A second Purim commandment is giving help to those in need. This is called tzedakah. People may **donate** money, food, or clothing.

A mishloach manot basket being received

Giving gifts of food to friends or family is another commandment. These gifts are called mishloach manot. They should include at least two types of food or drink. People make these baskets with fruit, juice, candy, and other treats.

The fourth Purim commandment is having a great feast. This joyful meal is called a seudah. It is shared with family and friends. People say prayers after the meal. The prayers thank God for food and **miracles**.

The seudah can include any foods people choose. Some families cook a meal with different meats. Others eat extra treats.

Meat and dishes for Purim

Purim Foods

One special Purim treat is hamantaschen. These are cookies with different fillings. They are shaped in a triangle like Haman's hat. Apricot, prune, and raspberry jelly are popular fillings.

The cookies can be baked at home or at synagogue. Dough is cut into circles. A spoonful of filling goes in the middle. Then each of the three corners are pinched into a triangle.

Other treats are common for Purim. Some people roll small strips of dough and fry them. Then they sprinkle the rolls with powdered sugar. These are meant to look like Haman's ears!

Rolled dough strips

Sambusak

Persian and Iraqi Jews enjoy turnovers called sambusak. They are another triangle-shaped food for Purim. These can be filled with meat, cheese, or chickpeas.

Purim Projects

You can make your own mishloach manot baskets for Purim. One idea is to fold an **origami** basket out of paper. You can also buy a basket or use one from home.

The next step is filling the baskets with different foods. Hamantaschen, oranges, tea bags, juice, fruit leather, and candy are popular choices. Some people also put a noisemaker inside. Now you are ready to give your baskets to friends and family!

Make cookies shaped like Haman's hat! Hamantaschen dough is simple. You can have fun with fillings. Pick your favorite fruit jelly. You can also try a sweet poppy seed filling. Chocolate chips or chocolate hazelnut spread are delicious too.

There are easy ways to make a Purim costume. Color a paper mask or decorate it with stickers. Make Haman's triangle hat or Queen Esther's crown out of paper. You can also use other costumes you already have. Superhero capes, princess dresses, and sports uniforms will all work.

Dress up. Tell the story of Esther. Help others. Have fun! It's Purim!

GLOSSARY

bravery (BRAY-vuh-ree)—having courage to face danger, fear, or difficulty

commandment (kuh-MAND-ment)—a rule or order someone has to follow

convince (kuhn-VINS)—to cause someone to believe or do something

donate (DOH-nayt) —to give something as a gift, especially to people who are in need

Hebrew (HEE-broo)—a language used by ancient Israelites and modern-day Jewish people

lunar (LOO-nuhr)—having to do with the moon

miracle (MEER-uh-kuhl)—an event that is seen as a result of God being involved in people's lives; miracles cannot be explained

origami (or-uh-GAH-mee)—the Japanese art of paper folding

rejoice (ri-JOYS)—to feel joy or great delight

synagogue (SIN-a-gog)—a building where Jewish people come together to pray

READ MORE

Last, Shari. *What Is Purim?* London, UK: Tell Me More Books, 2024.

Raij, Emily. *Jewish Festivals and Traditions.* North Mankato, MN: Capstone, 2025.

Raij, Emily. *We Gather at a Jewish Synagogue: A Place in Our Community.* North Mankato, MN: Capstone, 2025.

INTERNET SITES

Kiddle: Judaism Facts for Kids
kids.kiddle.co/Judaism

My Jewish Learning: Purim 101
myjewishlearning.com/article/purim-101

PJ Library: Celebrating Purim With Your Family
pjlibrary.org/purim

INDEX

ABOUT THE AUTHOR

Emily Raij has written more than 50 books for children and edited dozens of professional resources for K-12 teachers. She is a native of Chicago, where she earned her journalism degree from Northwestern University. She lives in Florida with her husband, daughter, son, and dog.